SUPER LARGE PRINT CROSSWORDS

EASY-TO-READ PUZZLES

SIRIUS

SIRIUS

This edition published in 2023 by Sirius Publishing, a division of
Arcturus Publishing Limited,
26/27 Bickels Yard, 151–153 Bermondsey Street,
London SE1 3HA

Copyright © Arcturus Holdings Limited
Puzzles by Puzzle Press

ISBN: 978-1-3988-3062-2
AD010923US

Printed in China

CONTENTS

PUZZLES..4

SOLUTIONS......................................82

1

Across

1 Eyes

5 "___ nice of you to ask": 2 wds.

10 Do damage to

11 Makeup company

12 Melville novel

13 Cottonwood trees

14 Watching carefully: hyph.

16 Hawaiian honker

17 Look at

21 Prison officer

23 Hwy. abbrs.

24 Friend in France

25 Live

26 Mount ___, peak on the border of Alberta and British Columbia

28 Metal fastening pin

31 Chinook salmon

32 Brontë heroine

33 Detailed examination

37 Singing group

40 "___ Fire" (Bruce Springsteen hit)

41 Final game in a trophy competition: 2 wds.

42 Prefix with technology

43 Peak

44 Vex, with "at"

Down

1 Cry of eagerness: hyph.

2 "___ Lama Ding Dong" (1961 hit)

3 Diet staple: 2 wds.

4 Preserved, in a way

5 Woman loved by Hercules

6 Swapper

7 Religious sch.

8 Part of many Brazilian place names

9 Certain football players, initially

11 Tier

15 Vane dir.

18 Respected leader in national or international affairs

19 Father in France

20 River of Flanders

21 Float, as an aroma

22 Soy sauce brand

27 Symbols of love

28 Cut out

29 Olive ____ (Popeye's lady)

30 Making an attempt

34 One night in Paris

35 College in New Rochelle

36 Winter whiteness

37 300, in old Rome

38 Charioteer of film: Ben-____

39 Unlock, in verse

2

Across

1 Some execs
5 Beer ingredient
9 "But you said…!" response: 2 wds.
11 "Sunset Blvd." actress Nancy
13 Iron: comb. form
14 Authority: hyph.
15 Dress up, with "out"
16 Author LeShan
18 Debate side
19 Braves outfielder Marrero
20 Coffee container
21 Garden tool
22 Cub Scout groups
24 Mergers
26 Letters to stars: 2 wds.
28 PGA Tour golfer Heath
30 Dark genre
33 Laughter syllable
34 Period of 100 yrs.
36 Slimy stuff
37 "Take Me Bak ____" (1972 Slade single)
38 California-based clothing brand, initially
39 Tags
40 1980 Carly Simon hit
42 In the work already quoted: abbr., 2 wds.
44 Prefix with venous or net
45 Alan Ladd classic
46 Bygone title
47 Robert who played A.J. Soprano

Down

1 Presented
2 Spanish chant: 2 wds.
3 Densely wooded areas in an untouched state: 2 wds.
4 Father's talk: abbr.
5 Exclamation of praise to God
6 Detroit Lions footballer Michael
7 Mental
8 "Already?": 2 wds.
10 "Mon ____!"
12 Ninth day in the ancient Roman calendar
17 Percussionist
23 Baglike structure

25 "Whom have ____ heaven but you?" Psalms 73:25: 2 wds.

27 Atomic

28 Japanese screen

29 Keen

31 Wound application

32 Roll-call list

35 Non-profit, voluntary citizens' groups, initially

41 Málaga Mrs.

43 Fraternity letter

3

Across

1 "The Planets" composer Gustav
6 Breakfast corners
11 Start of a clairvoyant's comment, perhaps: 3 wds.
12 Rear-___
13 Jazz trumpeter Ziggy
14 Heaths (Scot.)
15 Person on duty at a building's entrance
17 Organs of smell
18 "___ Network" (1980s comedy series)
20 Place for rings
25 Dirks of yore
27 Psalms interjection
28 Tricky catchers
30 Light and insubstantial
31 Silents star Bara
33 V.I.P.s, slangily: 2 wds.
38 ___ Wafers (cookie brand)
39 Espies
40 Certain language group
41 Complete reversal: hyph.
42 Vezina Trophy winner in 1994, 1995 and 1997
43 "Cómo ___?"

Down

1 Hightailed it
2 Capital city in Europe
3 Citrus drink: 2 wds.
4 Buccaneer: 2 wds.
5 Armored vehicles
6 Batman, to the Joker
7 "Movin' ___" ("The Jeffersons" theme song): 2 wds.
8 Dog in "Garfield" strips
9 "The King and I" co-star
10 Prom committee members: abbr.
16 Former Common Market inits.
18 Leaky balloon sound
19 "This is ___"
21 Adjusts anew
22 Empty: 2 wds.
23 Defunct org. that included Syria, initially
24 Far from the life of the party

26 Unfortunate happening that hinders

29 Doo-wop syllable

32 Go after

33 A Turner

34 Cutlass company, briefly

35 Ballet movement

36 Razor brand name

37 Form 1040 IDs

38 U.S. medical research agcy.

4

Across

1 Chef Lagasse
7 Kemo ____ (the Lone Ranger)
11 He moves diagonally in chess
12 Dog-eared
13 Came across
15 Historical land measures
16 Bother incessantly: 2 wds.
17 1814 Byron poem
18 Physicist Fermi
19 Tolkien creature
20 Weightlifting maneuver
21 "____ Secret" (Jefferson Airplane song): 2 wds.
22 Radiate from a central point: 2 wds.
24 "Platoon" setting, for short
27 Changeable
28 Two-wheeled vehicle
29 Boxer Ali
30 Not intoxicated
31 Not able to be described exactly
33 Long-running police drama series
34 Magnetic induction units
35 Police investigators, slangily
36 Loathe

Down

1 Big Band Era vocalist Ray
2 Bronze age civilization centered on Crete
3 Accompany to a party
4 TV's Morgenstern
5 Notes for those in debt, initially
6 Hosp. employee
7 Take an oath: 2 wds.
8 Of the body's main artery
9 Security error
10 Put an ____ (stop, as a rally): 2 wds.
14 Renter
18 Follow as a result
20 Minnesota arts college: 2 wds.
21 Out of the blue, perhaps

22 Man who is engaged to be married

23 Like vinegar

24 Eat like a rabbit

25 Cub Scout leaders, in the U.K.

26 Minimum

27 Ancient weapon material

28 "We're #1!," e.g.

30 Snick's partner

32 "___ be a pleasure!"

5

Across

1 "Really?": 2 wds.
5 Blackjack player's request: 2 wds.
10 Alpine sight
11 Not achieved
12 World Cup org.
13 "The Wind in the Willows" character: 2 wds.
14 Together, in music: 2 wds.
16 "Gross!" sounds
17 Large mass of land projecting into the sea
20 Publication detailing items for sale
21 Chew the fat
24 ___/IP
25 G.P.'s grp.
26 AOL rival
27 NASDAQ unit, shortly
28 Explosive powder, usually in strings
30 Cause the downfall of (usually a ruler)
32 Gator tail?
33 Nectar source
34 Plant-eating ground bug
36 Rice-a-___, the San Francisco treat
39 Caspar or Balthazar, e.g.
40 Talking horse of TV: 2 wds.
41 Yawning gulf
42 1975 Wimbledon champ

Down

1 World financial grp.
2 French pronoun
3 Talented child: 2 wds.
4 Bowls facilities
5 "Ben-___"
6 Celeron maker
7 Panels of glass that can be seen through from one side only: hyph., 2 wds.
8 Extinct flightless birds
9 Coda
13 Person with a compact, muscular body build
15 Loosen
17 Election numbers: abbr.
18 For one
19 "Casablanca" crook
22 Communiqué segue: 2 wds.

23 Had memorized

29 TV's "___ and Greg"

31 Second-nearest planet to the Sun

32 Ishmael's commander

34 Nashville-based awards org.

35 Author Lewis et al., initially

37 O.T. book

38 Chemical suffix

6

Across

1 Woodworking tool: hyph.
7 Dough dispenser, initially
10 Mark of a ruler: 2 wds.
11 Early gangsta rap collective inits.
12 Thin crisp biscuit: 2 wds.
14 ____ end (finished): 2 wds.
15 1997 N.L. Rookie of the Year Scott
16 "Looking for Mr. Goodbar" actor Richard
17 Check
18 Feminine ending
19 Begins
20 Pilgrim's destination, maybe
21 Lack of enthusiasm
23 Cubs' org.
26 Last day of the working week for many
27 Neither masc. nor fem.
28 Bank holdings: abbr.
29 And
30 Gillette product: 2 wds.
33 Prescription notation
34 Predetermined course of events
35 Sign of a smash, shortly
36 W.W. II torpedo ships: hyph.

Down

1 100-dollar bills, informally: hyph.
2 Evergreen conifers
3 Radio host Hansen
4 South African political party, initially
5 Computer program instruction: abbr.
6 Medicinal drug science
7 Short sock
8 Some suits
9 1914 and 1918 battle site
10 Indian tribe
13 Coconut flesh
17 "The Simpsons" mouse
19 Quash (a judgement): 2 wds.
20 Sketch show with Aries Spears and Michael McDonald: 2 wds.

21 William Tell, e.g.

22 Vagabond

23 Wisconsin city
or its college

24 Actress Sarandon
and singer Boyle

25 Skeleton, old-style

26 Abstains from food

27 Campaign issue
of 1992, initially

31 Lincoln's home, shortly

32 Aide in the Army, initially

7

Across

1 Former Eur. carrier
5 Difference in years between people: 2 wds.
11 "Young Frankenstein" role
12 Organ parts
13 Place where travelers are exploited: 2 wds.
15 Round juicy fruits
16 Property right
21 Pens
24 Roots used in poi
25 Hindu deity
26 Karate exercise
27 Region on the southeastern coast of China
29 Race of Norse gods
30 Coax with flattery
32 Toward the center
36 Casual outfit with a matching top and pants: 2 wds.
40 Full set of chromosomes
41 Sen. Cochran of Mississippi
42 Self-centeredness
43 Units of work

Down

1 ____-Honey (Mary Jane candy alternative): hyph.
2 ____ about (roughly): 2 wds.
3 Río contents
4 Semiprecious stone
5 Recesses with altars
6 Prepare (for): 2 wds.
7 N.J. summer setting
8 Long-jawed swimmer
9 Gulf Coast st.
10 Sony handheld device, initially
14 Certain food stores, initially
17 Be quick: 2 wds.
18 Historical chapters
19 Words of denial: 2 wds.
20 Russian emperor
21 Doorpost
22 "I've Got ____ in Kalamazoo": 2 wds.
23 Atahualpa, for one
28 Intense dislikes
29 Life ____ know it: 2 wds.
31 Like some legal proceedings: 2 wds.

33 Essen basin

34 Slantwise: abbr.

35 Criteria: abbr.

36 "T" size: abbr.

37 Head lines, for short?

38 Diminutive suffix, in Italian

39 "___ Married an Axe Murderer" (Mike Myers film): 2 wds.

8

Across

1 Japanese word meaning "circle"
5 "___ piacendo" (Italian for "God willing"): 2 wds.
9 Dallas suburb
11 Common sense?
12 Car insurer, initially
13 Ambles (along)
14 Parents, usually
16 Web letters in orange buttons
18 1598 French edict city
22 Absolutely
24 "Prince Valiant" cartoonist Foster
25 ___ Zedong
26 Abu Dhabi is its cap.
27 That, in Oaxaca
28 "It's cold!"
29 Intrudes suddenly
31 Providing weapons
33 Bag of chips, maybe
34 Original "Star Trek" actor
36 "___ Want to Dance?" Bobby Freeman hit: 2 wds.

39 ___ Swim, cable network
42 Several Russian tsars
43 Flexible Flyers
44 Keeps 'em in stitches?
45 To be, to Brutus

Down

1 Automobile sticker fig.
2 Kind of beer
3 Heavy shower
4 Remove from a box
5 Sitcom based in Harlem, "___ Andy": 2 wds.
6 Prefix meaning "ten": var.
7 Nouvelle Caledonie, e.g.
8 They protect QBs
10 Byname for South Africa's Paul Kruger ("Uncle")
11 Mister
15 Swell
16 Cuban ballroom dance
17 Beatle Ringo
19 Shane MacGowan and bandmates: 2 wds.
20 Bridge seats
21 Not just trim

23 Catastrophic

30 Working

32 Religious paintings: var.

35 "Life is Good" rapper

36 Insult, slangily

37 The ___ Glove (hot surface mitt)

38 Deviation

40 The Mormon church, for short

41 Lao-___

9

Across

1 Shaver
4 Singer Dion
10 Candid
12 Witness: 2 wds.
13 Kinnear of "The Kennedys"
14 Create a cryptogram
15 Owner of Menorca
17 Flowers, in Florence
19 19th Presidential initials
22 Long, straight-sided cigars
24 "Telephone Line" band, initially
25 It goes before E except after C: 2 wds.
26 "And," to Otto
27 Paronomasia
28 Marseilles Mrs.
29 "Bosom Buddies" star Peter
31 Massive Brit. lexicon
32 Minuscule, in slang
33 ___ Heaney, Irish poet who wrote "The Haw Lantern"
36 Big name in hotels
41 Head of Haiti
42 House of worship
43 Bygone blade
44 Bold poker words: 2 wds.
45 Defaces with rolls?: abbr.

Down

1 Box
2 Busy times at the I.R.S.
3 Like some food: hyph.
4 Event with big discounts: 2 wds.
5 One hundred million decades
6 ___ cit. (footnote abbr.)
7 Doubled, a Dixie Cups oldie about New Orleans
8 Go-ahead
9 WSW's reverse
11 New Zealand author Marsh
16 Neglect
18 "The Day ___" (Longfellow): 2 wds.
19 Act of returning money received previously
20 "Song 2" band
21 ___ soit qui mal y pense

22 Army fatigues, for short

23 Treater's phrase: 2 wds.

30 Exams for aspiring D.A.s

34 U.S. school near Juarez

35 Attends

36 Slugger's stat.

37 Atmospheric prefix

38 N.Y.C. subway inits.

39 Yellowfin, on Hawaiian menus

40 ____ Peres, Mo.

Across

1 Sketch comedy series inspired by a magazine: 2 wds.
6 Soup in Hanoi
9 Cache
10 "___ Calloways" (Disney film)
12 Member of the armed forces: 2 wds.
14 Runner Sebastian
15 Relative from Rio
16 It blinks and winks
17 Interpreter of Judaic law
19 Optical illusion often seen in deserts
22 Detective, at times
25 Advil rival
26 "The Faerie Queene" division
27 "And what ___ rare as a day…": 2 wds.
28 Boss, slangily: 2 wds.
29 Harmonious interval
31 Big ISP, once
33 Hothead's emotion
34 By means of
37 Shocking surprise
40 Hotsy-___

41 Appropriate forcibly
42 Cut
43 Bullfighting maneuvers

Down

1 Tiny time div.: 2 wds.
2 "… ___ additional cost to you!": 2 wds.
3 Charitable distribution
4 Annual opener
5 Trace
6 The third degree?
7 Country of origin
8 Start of "The Star Spangled Banner": 2 wds.
10 Dabbling duck
11 U-turn from WSW
13 Kitchen floor piece, perhaps
17 Mayhem
18 Military camp (Fr.)
19 Tai leader
20 French pronoun
21 Unwavering
23 "Who am ___ say?": 2 wds.
24 Cabin component
26 Attempt to hide a crime: hyph.

28 Container weight
30 Substantial, as a sum
31 Telecom letters
32 Cry of dismay: hyph.
34 Part of R.S.V.P.
35 "____ pastore" (opera by Mozart): 2 wds.
36 Biol. energy sources
38 Australian state whose capital is Sydney, initially
39 Jamboree grp.

11

Across

1 Seed again
6 Compound leaf of a fern
11 Small antelope
12 Actress Zellweger
13 Confine: 2 wds.
14 Lycee student
15 Actress Thompson of "Dear White People"
17 "Me! Me! Me!": 2 wds.
18 He lost at Gettysburg
20 "Na-Nu Na-Nu" sayer, e.g.
22 Elite groups: hyph.
24 R&B singer Erykah
27 Gold dealer's unit
28 Sci-fi and horror writer Bob
29 Jedi antagonist in "Star Wars"
30 Medicine cabinet item
31 Funnyman Youngman
33 T-shirt sizes: abbr.
34 Seek a seat
36 Drag one's feet
38 Causing difficulty in breathing
40 Being prostrate
43 Wear, as clothing: 2 wds.
44 Brook or lake fish
45 Series about the Cohens, Coopers and Nichols: 2 wds.
46 Greek-American musician whose albums include "Inspirato"

Down

1 Defraud
2 Ending for ranch or haban
3 Semiquaver: 2 wds.
4 Actor's award
5 Naively charming
6 Flip (out)
7 Pastor's field: abbr.
8 Rare person or thing: 4 wds.
9 River that flows from Lake Ladoga to the Gulf of Finland
10 Hold
16 Promgoers: abbr.
18 Country, capital Vientiane
19 Pin holder
21 Sacked out
23 Distress signal
25 "Curses!"

26 Ones in France
28 Allegiance
30 CD earnings
32 "No Strings Attached" band
34 Proof of purchase: abbr.

35 "That's a lie!": hyph.
37 Vega's constellation
39 "Kitchy-___!"
41 Agnes of "Agnes of God," for one
42 Volkswagen model

12

Across

1 Parting words, briefly
6 Ballpark figs.
10 Group of nine
11 Grafting shoot
12 Sentimental person, informally
13 Now
14 Fraternal letter
15 Charley of the 1960s Orioles
17 Airport schedule letters
18 Many moons
19 School grouping in some states, initially
20 Forego folding
21 Coconut fiber
23 Smoked herring
25 Layer of earth on the surface
27 Have an unpleasant odor: 2 wds.
29 Emulate yeast-bread
32 Coin flip call: abbr.
33 Joke response, initially
35 Officer who looks into motor vehicle collision fatalities
36 French affirmative
37 Lyrical Gershwin
38 1960s chess champ
39 Ladies of the house, informally
41 Paris's river
43 Full of chutzpah
44 Bellybutton variety, slangily
45 Indolent
46 Sci-fi author Janet

Down

1 With hopes of being sold: 2 wds.
2 Blubber
3 Immeasurably small
4 Asian occasion
5 Do a do
6 Green
7 Extremely amusing
8 Just so: 3 wds.
9 Late talk show host Tom
11 Kind of apartment
16 Demands: 2 wds.
22 Seoul soldier, initially
24 Area of a circle = ____-squared: 2 wds.
26 Buff

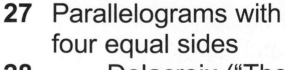

27 Parallelograms with four equal sides

28 ___ Delacroix ("The Green Mile" protagonist)

30 Singer Twain whose albums include "Up!"

31 Former space shuttle commander Collins

34 Corrective eye surgery

40 Enzyme suffix

42 Bambi's aunt

13

Across

1 A whole lot
5 How some songs are sold: 2 wds.
10 TV host with a role in "The Color Purple"
12 12
13 ___ citato (in the work cited)
14 Alamogordo's county
15 Boundary, briefly
16 Org. that helps with motel discounts
18 Jaguar or Jeep
19 Nibbled on
20 Jean-___ Godard (French-Swiss director)
21 Chart topper
22 Jekyll's counterpart
24 30th anniversary gifts
26 Prepare to fence direction: 2 wds.
28 Big name in fashion
30 On ___ (equipotent): 2 wds.
33 Scenic Scottish river
34 Wall St. wheeler-dealer
36 Japanese vegetable
37 CPO's outfit

38 ID-assigning org.
39 Coiled choker
40 Lewd character
42 Furnaces for firing pottery
44 Snicker: hyph.
45 Member of an Eastern church
46 Bygone blades
47 Handel opera, "___ and Galatea"

Down

1 Cabbage
2 Presumptuously arrogant
3 Peppermint-flavored liqueur: 3 wds.
4 Part of a guffaw
5 First barbarian king of Italy
6 Negating particle
7 European country: 2 wds.
8 Divert (a process) from its intended course
9 Is audibly derisive
11 Patch up
17 Home-helpers from abroad: 2 wds.
23 "Bambi" character

25 Programming language based on Pascal

27 Grinds, as teeth

28 Full-price payers

29 Like cult films, again and again

31 My Lord, in Hebrew

32 Prepares coffee grounds

35 Azerbaijan's capital

41 Bee follower

43 ____ moment: 2 wds.

14

Across

1 Terhune title "Lad: ____": 2 wds.
5 "The final frontier"
10 "Whip It" band
11 Criticize harshly: 2 wds.
12 "New Jack City" rapper-actor: hyph.
13 Old-style form of transport
14 Henner of "Taxi"
16 Place for a pad
17 Black mark
19 HST's successor
21 "____, I've had enough!": 2 wds.
25 "Hath ____ sister?" (Shakespeare): 2 wds.
26 W.W. II org.
27 Atlas abbr.
28 Makeshift arrangements: hyph.
30 U.S. Army medal
31 "Lawrence of Arabia" star
33 TV interviewer who called astronaut "Buzz" Aldrin "Buzz Lightyear": 2 wds.
36 Agreed-upon facts
39 Insect with hard wing cases
41 Arizona river
42 Name
43 Calif.-Fla. route: 2 wds.
44 Heads overseas?
45 Drag racing org.

Down

1 Take ____ view of: 2 wds.
2 Numerical prefix
3 In a foreign country
4 "Aha!": 2 wds.
5 "Wailing" instrument: abbr.
6 Find fault with: 2 wds.
7 Thicke, Turing or Tudyk
8 Feel concern
9 Kitchen suffix
11 Uncouth in speech: hyph.
15 Departed quickly: 2 wds.
18 Vintner Paul
19 World's largest logistics company, initially
20 Bona ____ (goddess also called Fauna)
22 Stand up for: 2 wds.
23 Magazine no.

24 Letters of concern
29 Immobilize, at a rodeo: hyph.
32 Gain computer access: 2 wds.
33 Blind as ____: 2 wds.

34 ____-humanité
35 Suffix with cheer or cheek
37 Marlin or Cardinal, e.g.
38 Yemen's capital: var.
40 T-shirt sizes: abbr.

15

Across

1 Pinched: 2 wds.
6 Bounty
11 Home of the University of Maine
12 Pull again, say
13 Divine name in showbiz: 2 wds.
14 Blot out
15 Popular drink name from 1898–1961: hyph.
17 Turkish bath-house
18 "Terrible" Russian ruler
20 Lens settings: hyph.
24 ____ vivant
25 Actor Hakeem ____-Kazim, Colonel Iké Dubaku in "24"
26 Original, in Oberammergau
27 Infuriate
29 Brutus's "Behold!"
30 Traveling, as a band: 2 wds.
32 Having wide interests or abilities: hyph.
35 City in northeastern India
36 Ore deposits
38 Road through the Twin Cities: 2 wds.
39 Some native New Yorkers
40 Celestial bodies
41 January 21, May 8, October 30, et. al.

Down

1 It's measured in MB
2 Doesn't give ____: 2 words
3 Part of a horse's bridle
4 From wing to wing
5 Food label phrase: 2 wds.
6 Exact
7 Transplant
8 Type type: abbr.
9 ____ Nostra
10 Lea lady
16 Babies
18 "Think" sloganeer
19 Radio org.
21 With an arrangement to pay later: 2 wds.
22 Chest muscle, briefly
23 Go after
25 Mombasa residents

28 "Lethal Weapon" director Richard

29 Oprah's character in "The Princess and the Frog"

31 Lubricated

32 A sloop has one

33 "Girl" lead-in

34 ____-Lite, group whose albums include "World Clique"

35 Boil fluid

37 Snake's sound

16

Across

1 Five Norse kings
6 Little bit, in slang
11 David Copperfield's field
12 Milk: prefix
13 Kindly: hyph.
15 Ancient theaters
16 ___ Fail, Irish coronation stone
17 Stout glove
22 Family of languages
25 Compass reading, initially
26 Place on top of, overlay
29 Degree from Cranbrook Academy, initially
30 Reached inside and searched
31 Sheep breed of Colombia and Venezuela
34 Long. crosser
35 Fizz kicker
39 Suitable for or occupied by houses
43 Aromatic solvent
44 Exploits
45 Magna cum ___
46 Greek twenty prefix

Down

1 Sequel to "Typee"
2 Californian law enforcement agency letters
3 "A Death in the Family" writer
4 Wangle
5 Coll., e.g.
6 Assassinated
7 Measure of purity, for gold
8 Fall mo.
9 Véronique, for one: abbr.
10 Brick-carrying trough
14 Make free from confusion and ambiguity
18 Put on TV
19 10th-century pope: 2 wds.
20 Start of Massachusetts' motto
21 Irate, with "off"
22 Department of Transportation agcy.
23 Starched frill worn around the neck
24 On ___ with: 2 wds.
27 Fellas

28 Manmade material

32 "But you told me that…" retort: 2 wds.

33 Inner circle

36 Disney's "____ & Stitch"

37 Acorn bearers

38 Designer Schiaparelli

39 Family mem.

40 Hippocrates' H

41 Moo ____ pork

42 Abbr. between a first and last name, maybe

17

Across

1 Specialized market
6 Love, in Eire
9 Smear
11 Pigeon-___
12 Like topiary
13 "___ Bowl of Tea" (Wayne Wang movie): 2 wds.
14 Bills, e.g.
15 Parody
17 Prefix with meter
18 With regard to
19 Plaintiff's opposite, briefly
20 Grooms' mates
21 Praises vociferously
23 It's a wrap
26 Specialized computer, for short
30 "There's ___ Goin' On" (Sly and the Family Stone album): 2 wds.
31 Mont Blanc, par exemple
32 Scientific research critter: 2 wds.
34 Family
35 Rhyme scheme pattern
36 Long-distance walkers
38 Comrade in arms
39 Real: 2 wds.
40 It's not quite lge.
41 Aquatic mammal

Down

1 Winston Cup org.
2 Breathe
3 Sea shores
4 Words of approval: 3 wds.
5 Wind dir.
6 Spurred
7 Alter the pitch of (an instrument)
8 Adjusts to one's situation
10 N.F.L. stats
11 Item needed on court: 2 wds.
16 Bowling great Anthony
20 Huge
22 Architectural pier

23 Hello, in Arabic

24 Fit for farming

25 Like vulgar humor

27 Most indisposed

28 Scant

29 Ceremonial burner

33 Meteorologist's comfort meas.

37 Rescuer of Odysseus, in myth

18

Across

1 The same, in Sevres
6 Laser light
10 Arsène ___, crime fiction character
11 Black ink item
13 Bass instrument
15 Suffix with rep or rev
16 Rapper Tone ___
17 Suffix with Capri
18 Genetics lab. study
19 Like some curves: hyph.
21 "___ Smile" (Hall & Oates song)
23 Mathematician who introduced the symbol e for the base of natural logarithms
24 Budweiser rival
26 Container for refining a metal
28 Barre des Écrins, par exemple
32 Good-for-nothing person
34 It can start with "http"
35 It comes before long
36 Antipoverty agcy.
37 Main
38 They assist senior military officers: hyph.
41 No longer out, in a way
42 Rouses
43 Detergent target
44 Get around

Down

1 Glass eels
2 French ___ (South American department)
3 Like some nerve cells
4 Short, for short
5 Organic compounds
6 Dionysus
7 Jargon suffix
8 Not even
9 Foundry worker
12 Struck with the outer end of the head of a golf club
14 Common name for the medical condition epistaxis
20 Resort near Snowbird
22 Datebook entry: abbr.

25 Type of can
26 Dental decay
27 Comfortable with: 2 wds.
29 Capital of Zambia
30 Drug given before an operation: abbr.

31 Go by, as time
32 Become tiresome
33 "Camelot" composer
39 "____ tu" (aria for Renato)
40 The NBA's Walt Frazier, briefly

19

Across

1 Shocked with a device
6 Bakery treat
11 Sharp, as pain
12 Do a lube job on: 2 wds.
13 Charger's array
14 Diarist Nin
15 Small alteration
17 Ruler of Kuwait, e.g.
18 Mena of "American Beauty"
22 Kind of race
26 Bridget Riley's genre: 2 wds.
27 Roman numeral for 2012
28 French bench
29 Fall or summer
30 Place for portraits
32 Apply new paint and wallpaper
38 Mischief makers' denial: 2 wds.
39 Cache
40 Talk show host Lake
41 Out of favor (with): 2 wds.
42 Son of Jacob
43 Ancient burial chambers

Down

1 "Look what I did!": hyph.
2 Didn't just pass
3 Theme or topic: abbr.
4 Ides rebuke: 2 wds.
5 Pie or pudding
6 "Ditto!": 3 wds.
7 Widescreen filmmaking technique
8 ___ Montgomery, pop-art portraitist
9 Ravel's "Gaspard de la ___"
10 Some music purchases, for short
16 "Stop telling me these things!," initially
18 Weep uncontrollably
19 Work ___ sweat: 2 wds.
20 Moving need
21 Prince of the former ruling house of Austria
23 Pharm. paperwork
24 "Liquid Water Enhancer" brand
25 Disappoint a father
27 Musical

29 Utah's capital, initially

31 Race of Norse gods

32 French for "kings"

33 Cut

34 Painter Guido ____

35 Cop calls, initially

36 Exactly: 3 wds.

37 Approximate takeoff times, for short

38 F.D.R.-era agcy.

20

Across

1 LAX data
5 Aligned: 3 wds.
11 Avoid
12 Bug
13 "God Help the Child" author Morrison
14 Typewriter feature: 2 wds.
15 Rare blood type: abbr., 2 wds.
16 Suffix with pay
17 Cry like a sheep
19 Pants, slangily
23 Uses an adhesive: 2 wds.
26 Med. drama sites
27 Without a ____ stand on: 2 wds.
28 Org.
30 Sigourney's "Ice Storm" director
31 Murdering
33 Divisions of a week
35 Adams of "Octopussy"
36 Medical provider grp.
38 Exec's note
41 Russian coin: var.
44 ____ B'rith

45 "____ Girl" (Trey Songz song): 3 wds.
46 O.T. book
47 So very much
48 Roger of "Nicholas Nickleby"

Down

1 "Cómo ____?"
2 End of some fundraisers?
3 Beach vehicle: 2 wds.
4 Humorous, made-up word
5 Altogether: 2 wds.
6 Oscar-winning Patricia
7 Chance for a hit: 2 wds.
8 Some linemen: abbr.
9 "Hooray!"
10 Covered with beads, maybe
18 "Dilbert" intern
20 Somewhere to live
21 "Off ____?": 2 wds.
22 SOS responders
23 Bag brand
24 Chanteuse Horne
25 "The Lion King" lioness

29 Insomniac's wish

32 "Everything's fine": 2 wds.

34 Like some pantyhose

37 1450, to Caesar

39 Medieval weapon

40 Alternative to acrylics

41 Joke around with

42 Divisor for any prime number

43 Royal insomnia cause

21

Across

1 Type of PC image
7 Till bill
10 Founder of est, Werner ____
11 "Deadwood" airer
12 Small cart used in building-work
14 Civics, e.g.
15 Penlight battery, initially
16 Olive genus
17 Clouded up
18 Hospital V.I.P.s
19 Pianist Jarrett and others
21 ____ mignon
22 Some Ford models, for short: hyph.
24 Nian Rebellion general
27 Office correspondence
28 Gorilla researcher Fossey
29 Latin wife
30 Third stomach of a ruminant
32 Redeeming quality or characteristic: 2 wds.
34 Here, in Paris
35 Fur source
36 Cedar Rapids college
37 Rejector of a proposal

Down

1 See with attention
2 Tony winner Worth and others
3 Bara of the silents
4 ____ fide (in bad faith)
5 Wall St. figures
6 HTC phone, e.g.
7 Pummel
8 W.W. II torpedo ships: hyph.
9 "Forget it!": 2 wds.
12 "To ____ It May Concern:"
13 "Have a Heart" singer
17 Architect ____ van der Rohe
19 White wine apéritifs
20 Antiquity, in antiquity
21 Pasta similar to rotelle
22 Gas station name
23 No Oscar winner: hyph.
24 Medicinal decoction

25 Cup holder

26 Tab grabber's words: 2 wds.

27 Songs and such

28 "Deep Red" director, ___ Argento

30 Bugbear

31 Band with the 2010 album "Congratulations"

33 Ariz. adjoiner

22

Across

1 Cry like a cat
5 Latin 101 word
9 Maker of Stylus Pro printers
11 Bud holder
12 Poetry without rhyme: 2 wds.
14 Pro opposite
15 Aromatic root credited with medicinal properties
17 Car co. bought by Chrysler
18 A.C. stat
19 Hwy.
20 Brit. honors
22 Religious leader
24 Excuse
26 Childish talk: hyph.
29 Slow Churned ice cream
33 Previous work: abbr.
34 "Treasure Island" initials
36 Bolivian president Morales
37 Solid part of a fat
39 "Plop" preceder

40 Regard something as likely
42 Tennis Hall-of-Famer Nastase
43 Animal hides
44 Cleaning cabinet supplies
45 Scoffer's snort: 2 wds.

Down

1 Internet video tool
2 Poise
3 Time allowance for bill payment
4 First name in horror films
5 Alphabet City street: 2 wds.
6 "Curiosity" rover's destination
7 Declare
8 Taken care of: 2 wds.
10 1940s Soviet state security org.
13 Filled with malice
16 E.U. language: abbr.
21 Slump
23 Inc., overseas
25 British trucks

26 Some appliances, for short

27 Beefy soup ingredient

28 For all to see

30 City of northern Illinois: 2 wds.

31 Actress Mimieux

32 Most mad

35 Barbershop sound

38 Play to ___, draw: 2 wds.

41 Province east of N.B.

23

Across

1 Italian brandy
7 Code breakers' org.
10 Make again, as a map
11 Flavor ___ (rapper)
12 Port city on Humboldt Bay
13 Town on the Connecticut River
14 Thrift shop warning: 2 wds.
15 Natural spring that gives out steam
17 Golf's Ballesteros
18 Old Apple computers
19 Adam's apple location
20 Be generous
21 Pluck
23 Rectangle with four right angles
26 Uno y dos y tres
30 Parisian aunt
31 Car bar
32 Diet doctor
34 Five-time winners of the Rose Bowl, initially
35 Hand in Hidalgo
36 Certain prejudice or discrimination
38 Part of speech of the word "I" or "it": abbr.
39 Summer drink: 2 wds.
40 Go unused
41 "Sesame ___" (kids' show)

Down

1 Thick oily substance
2 Brought back into play
3 Where floppy disks went: 2 wds.
4 Appearance
5 Neighbor of Afghanistan, briefly
6 Like gossiping tongues
7 Actress Milano
8 Attacked: 2 wds.
9 Not disposed (to)
11 E.T. craft: 2 wds.
16 North Carolina school
20 Daniel ___ Kim, founder of 3AD
22 Creature with the scientific name Troglodytes troglodytes

23 Brings the foot down heavily

24 Native of Doha

25 Disentangle

27 Bring a thrill to

28 "Maybe": 2 wds.

29 Marine creature forming mossy colonies: 2 wds.

33 Hindu titles

37 Pretend

24

Across

1 P.T.A. interest, briefly
5 Fuel pipe closer: 2 wds.
11 Dermatology study
12 Football Hall-of-Famer Jim
13 Dyspepsia
15 Irish county
16 Fuel brand with green and white stations
17 Spanish queens
20 Alsatian sounds
23 Lens settings: hyph.
26 Shaving cream alternative
27 Sot's sound
28 ___ Today
29 Close the deal: 2 wds.
31 Elec. company, e.g.
32 Arrives home: 2 wds.
34 Place to be picked up?
36 City in Finland
40 Ed Harris's "Nixon" role: 3 wds.
43 Landlocked African country
44 1960s TV boy
45 Did as one was told
46 Charted information

Down

1 ___ the Red (Norwegian explorer)
2 Pioneer Boone, familiarly
3 Stamp of approval, initially
4 Cricket sounds
5 Pioneer cell phone co.
6 Magic show reactions
7 Having the effect of: 2 wds.
8 Calls: 2 wds.
9 Army mail centers, initially
10 Sharpies, e.g.
14 "Is that so!"
18 "___ Tuesday, This Must Be Belgium": 2 wds.
19 Foreign policy gp.
20 McGrath and McGranery, for short
21 Suffix for chicka or campo
22 Pennant-hoisting site
24 Letter before omega
25 Actor Mineo
27 Chart maker
30 Latitude
31 Shoeless

33 Roadside bomb letters

34 "The Mysterious Island" captain

35 1956 Peck role

37 Insect stage

38 "I'm ___!" ("Right away!"): 2 wds.

39 Traditional dance from Tahiti

41 Cause of speechlessness

42 Clean

25

Across

1 "Concerto ___" George Gershwin composition: 2 wds.
4 Where mil. planes land
7 Menlo Park monogram
8 Real, cutesy-style
9 It has a prominent goatee
12 E.M.T.'s skill
13 Actress Ann-___
15 Warning devices
17 Mutt
18 "On the Waterfront" director Kazan
19 Il ___, title assumed by Mussolini
20 Dinnerware washer
24 NATO member, briefly
25 Resistant to guidance or discipline
27 "Now I get it!"
29 Ultimate client for which a thing is intended: 2 wds.
32 Follower of three- or pigeon-
34 Lab burner
35 Fine-tune
37 "Hamlet" courtier
38 Bottoms of crankcases: 2 wds.
40 Sugar finish
41 French possessive
42 Papeete's island: abbr.
43 Airline to Eindhoven, initially
44 "Wheel of Fortune" purchase: 2 wds.
45 Wide spec.

Down

1 Had a strong urge to do something
2 City on the Tyrrhenian Sea
3 Rides at the expo: 2 wds.
4 24-hour bank features, shortly
5 Italian brother
6 Pat on the back?
9 Certain tennis return: 2 wds.
10 Clark Bar manufacturer
11 King Arthur's father
14 Creator and ruler of the universe
16 Okinawa port
21 Deli bread

22 Wheat covering
23 "Yikes!"
26 Cries over
27 Hahn and Klemperer
28 Mandel of "Deal
or No Deal"

30 Isolate
31 Flower part
33 Skip of a stone on water
36 Martial arts exercise
37 Sumo wrestling move
39 Bert Bobbsey's twin sister

26

Across

1 Some computer keys
7 "My ___" (#1 hit for the Knack)
9 Freelancer's enc.
12 Plant used to poison Socrates
13 South end?
14 Abate
15 Lassie, for example
17 Not smooth or level
20 "I won't take ___ an answer": 2 wds.
21 Russian whip
23 Vision: prefix
24 Awakens: 2 wds.
26 Abbr. after many a general's name
28 Arena seating sections
30 Indigo-yielding shrubs
32 Romain de Tirtoff's, familiarly
34 Insurance giant founded in 1871
36 "The Crying Game" star
37 Gave de ___, French river

38 Arctic jackets
41 Part of O.H.M.S.
42 Tots
43 Dough of flour, shortening and water

Down

1 Peter of Peter and Gordon
2 South African antelope
3 Boisterous, slangily
4 Florida airport letters
5 Lure to love
6 1960s civil rights org.
8 "Locked Up" singer
9 Like many works by Albrecht Dürer: hyph.
10 "I Predict ___" (song by Kaiser Chiefs): 2 wds.
11 Febrero preceder
16 Civil disturbance criminal
18 Considerable in size
19 Run smoothly
22 Hanoi holiday
25 Thou, to a frau
26 Chief Wiggum's son on "The Simpsons"

27 Zhou ___, prime minister of China 1949–76

29 It, in a playground game

31 Badlands state: abbr., 2 wds.

33 Full of lip

35 Bit

39 ___ Mae Brown (Whoopi Goldberg's "Ghost" role)

40 Places for forks: abbr.

27

Across

1 Shed tears
6 Karmann-___ (sports car)
10 Less common
11 Have ___ for (be naturally talented in): 2 wds.
12 Period of one's life
14 Fairy queen
15 D.C. school named for a president
16 Lamb's sound
17 One who's "just looking"
19 Ending for a school of thought
20 Greek bone
21 ___ crust (outer layer of our planet)
23 "Heavens to ___!"
25 Submit
28 Columbia org.
32 Brooklyn, e.g.: abbr.
33 Flips
35 "Wheel of Fortune" purchase: 2 wds.
36 Piece of pipe
37 Go-___ (1980s band)

38 Beginning piano student's exercise: 3 wds.
41 Race that includes Odin, Thor, and Balder
42 Starbucks sizes
43 Rare blood type, informally: 2 wds.
44 Grenoble girlfriends

Down

1 Rhyming word game
2 Airplane locators
3 Isaac Asimov classic: 2 wds.
4 Fish found in sushi restaurants
5 Grounds
6 Rap group based in Southern Chicago
7 Weed with purplish flowers
8 One way to pay: 2 wds.
9 Elite groups: hyph.
11 Popular Hondas
13 Sugar, e.g.
18 "Can ___ friends?": 2 wds.
22 1984 NL MVP Sandberg

24 Globe position?
25 1981 Genesis album
26 Cheats: 2 wds.
27 Clothes line?
29 Large wild sheep of Asia

30 1966 U.S. Open champion Fred
31 Size up
34 Roman hearth goddess
39 Dance in compound time
40 Ending for web or video

28

Across

1 Some ones in France?
5 Tony and Emmy
11 "And ___ bed" (Pepys): 2 wds.
12 They observe and keep records
13 Common suffix to Japanese ship names
14 Double dealing
15 1988 John Mellencamp song: 2 wds.
17 Comedian in "The Ministry of Silly Walks" sketch
18 Most eager to do something new
21 Donald Duck's nephews, e.g.
24 Modern courtroom evidence letters
25 "Started" in poetry
26 Dimensions
28 Circus clown Kelly
31 Magical drink
33 Estate where sugar is grown, for example
37 Last month
38 Like some Chardonnay
39 Midday meeting, slangily
40 Ending for teen
41 Coming
42 Birdbrain

Down

1 Letters at Camp Lejeune
2 Ancient mariner
3 French existentialist's word
4 Lake Itasca, to the Mississippi
5 "But still…": 2 wds.
6 "___ unto him who …": 2 wds.
7 Not marked up: 2 wds.
8 Come out again
9 Bit
10 Concorde letters
16 "Treasure Island" inits.
18 Dept. store stuff
19 DiFranco of pop
20 "Congratulations!"
22 "Am ___ risk?": 2 wds.
23 N.Y. neighbor
27 "Seinfeld" gal
28 Blackmail
29 One to remember, for short

30 "The Wind in the Willows" character: 2 wds.

32 "____ this blunder still you find" (Hannah More): 2 wds.

33 Walk wearily

34 Othello's false friend

35 Agreed to, slangily

36 Laura who wrote "Eli's Comin'"

37 ____ corda (musical direction)

29

Across

1 Not many: 2 wds.
5 Prefix with nuclear
11 Mother of Reuben, Simeon, Levi and Judah
12 Trix-craving critter
13 Florida's ___ Beach
14 Lacking in pigment
15 Ally McBeal, e.g.: abbr.
16 Goes by
17 Basketball, in slang
19 Quiet and reserved
21 Stock market index
24 Poetic homage
25 City, informally
27 "She" in Portuguese
28 Literary contraction
29 Democratic way of assigning chores: 2 wds.
31 "Casablanca" actor
32 Opens up at the doctor's office, perhaps?: 2 wds.
36 It has a low pH
39 Not damaged by use, weather, etc.
40 Govt. investigative org.
41 Empty space or area
42 Big name in computers
43 Lost freshness
44 Sultana's chambers

Down

1 Menlo Park middle name
2 Karate weapons
3 Those who live on our planet, in sci-fi
4 "___ gonna call? Ghostbusters!": 2 wds.
5 Show spun off of "M*A*S*H": 3 wds.
6 Charter member of the Pro Football Hall of Fame
7 Drops off
8 Diamond stats
9 Coal site
10 Siouan people
18 Sch. in Tulsa, Oklahoma
19 Buck's mate
20 Dutch city
21 Marked by low spirits
22 Slangy suffix
23 More than a battle

26 Queens, e.g.: abbr.

30 "Apocalypse Now" star Marlon

31 Lash ____ of old westerns

32 Explorer, Safari, and Navigator, e.g.

33 Med. school class

34 Blue Triangle org.

35 Essence

37 ____ Mujeres, Mexico

38 Sluggers' hits: abbr.

30

Across

1 Long Island airport
6 "Beowulf" beverage
10 Exotic jelly flavor
11 Belgian battle site
13 Doubt
15 Part of some e-mail addresses
16 Mil. rank achieved by Buzz Aldrin
17 Always, to Yeats
18 Underwater construction worker
20 Cable company that merged with AT&T in 1999
21 Cook quickly, like tuna
22 Ray of "GoodFellas"
24 Hindu spiritual life principle
26 Sighter of the Pacific Ocean, 1513
29 Axis of ____
33 Clark's "Mogambo" co-star
34 Visible horizon
36 Actor Cariou
37 Palmer's pedestal
38 Cape Town's land, initially
39 ____ of Independence
42 Golfer Sam
43 French explorer La ____
44 Senorita's other
45 Like some jackets

Down

1 Comment said with shrugged shoulders: 2 wds.
2 Ice cream parlor order
3 Gap
4 "____ Got a Secret"
5 Roast slightly
6 Muscular pain
7 Prefix with cycle
8 Newsman Peter
9 Discern
12 Aleppo's land
14 Person who produces manufacturing implements
19 Blah
23 Scott Turow's first book: 2 wds.
25 Deep-fried pancake topped with beans, etc.

26 Gets bare on top
27 Johnson & Johnson subsidiary
28 Surgeon's tool
30 Very manly
31 Boot part

32 Listed
35 Bakery supply
40 Gibbon of Thailand and Malaysia
41 Choice marble

31

Across

1 Make a collar
4 "It's c-c-cold!"
7 Highest note in Guido's scale
8 ____ Jemison (first African American woman in space)
9 Health resort
12 Internet location
14 ____ Grosbard, director of "True Confessions"
15 "Foxfire" author Seton
16 "Sure!": 2 wds.
18 Dance music genre
20 One may get pins and needles
21 Everyone who chooses to take part
23 Early role-playing game co., initially
25 Furnace fuel
26 Butt
27 More scraggy
30 Reagan cabinet member
31 Cochise portrayer of 1950s TV, Michael ____
34 Eastern hospice for travelers
36 Lennon's in-laws
37 "Dark Souls," e.g.
38 Foolish
40 Bow
41 Dawn goddess
42 Small island
43 Snow, in Scotland
44 Super ____ (GameCube predecessor)

Down

1 Not yet used to: 2 wds.
2 Coeur d'____
3 Vehicle you can push your infant in: 2 wds.
4 Performance rights org.
5 Logical and methodical reasoning
6 Casting need
9 Below ground
10 Membrane enveloping a lung
11 Psychologist's study
13 Satirist Mort
17 Moon lander, for short
19 Sweet ____, brand of artificial sweetener: 2 wds.
22 "Chocolat" actress

23 Rock concert souvenir: hyph.

24 Shrimp ____

28 Farm-related: abbr.

29 Class for foreigners, for short

32 "____ the Riveter" (W.W. II icon)

33 Aides: abbr.

35 Cote denizens

39 Org. doing pat-downs

32

Across

1 Prince Valiant's wife
6 Mawkish
11 Maj.'s superior: 2 wds.
12 Martinique mountain
13 Trailer: abbr.
14 "___ Ben Johnson" (inscription on a tomb): 2 wds.
15 Form 1040 datum
16 Massenet opera
18 Just like that!
19 Prefix with centenary
22 Freelance fighter
24 "Coming of Age in Samoa" author Margaret
26 Department of France
27 Claim
31 FBI worker, for short
32 One of "The Avengers"
33 Cantilevered window
35 "Polythene ___" (Beatles song)
38 Long-gone, as times
40 Brazilian actress Sonia
42 Good, to Galileo
43 Attempt to win a contest
44 Old laborers
45 California border lake

Down

1 Liechtenstein's locale
2 Written communications: abbr.
3 Greenspan's subj.
4 Actor Arnold
5 Puerto Rican baseball players' family name
6 Mooch
7 Soaring starter
8 Banana-like fruit with green skin
9 In accordance with
10 "___-haw!"
17 Mandela's org.
18 Eliot novel, "Adam ___"
20 Some TV drama sets
21 Bread used for a Reuben sandwich
22 Extinct elephantlike mammal
23 Breakfast dining area
24 Plaintive cry
25 Perry Mason creator's initials
28 Safari sights, briefly
29 Day between Mon. and Wed.

30 "Yeah, right!": 2 wds.
34 French president and prime minister, Jacques ___ Chirac
35 Approach
36 Farm prefix

37 Lee ___, Major League Baseball player (1959–71)
38 Award bestowed by Queen Eliz.
39 Light units: abbr.
41 Genetic material initials

33

Across

1 Native Nigerians
5 Certain mites
10 Flat
11 Breakfast sizzler
12 High spot
13 Cute ___ be: 2 wds.
14 Boner
15 "It's ___ thing" (easy winner): 2 wds.
16 Dissents
17 Kinds
18 TV show with skits
19 Actor Eastwood
22 Chemical element of atomic No. 52
25 Legendary baseball exec Bill
26 Spanish king
28 "...blackbirds baked in ___": 2 wds.
30 MS. enclosure
31 Al ___
33 Soaks
34 Race that includes Odin, Thor, and Balder
35 Political pawn González
36 Doesn't exactly sprint
37 Shell alternative
38 Belief
39 Chi follower

Down

1 Repeating
2 Director of "Diner" and "Rain Man": 2 wds.
3 Mixtures
4 Palm reader, e.g.
5 Quatrain rhyme scheme, sometimes
6 Gossip columnist Igor ("Cholly Knickerbocker")
7 Adoption of customs, beliefs, etc.
8 "Masters Without Slaves" author
9 Mystery author Michael
10 Composer Saint-___
19 Suffix for ventri or vehi
20 "Star Trek" captain, Jean-___ Picard
21 Aggravate

23 It flows with the wind: 2 wds.

24 Taylor of "Designing Women"

27 Easy type of question: 2 wds.

28 Accommodate

29 John Thomas ____, portrait painter

30 Game ragout

32 Previously, once

33 Laser path

34

Across

1 Put a new price on, say
6 Augmentation: abbr.
10 Co-Nobelist Sadat
11 China's Zhou ___
12 People chiefly responsible for the execution of a plan: 2 wds.
14 "Am ___ your way?": 2 wds.
15 Creator of Jeffy, Dolly and Barfy
16 "How to Succeed in Business Without Really Trying" librettist Burrows
17 Arrhythmia detector letters
18 1988 NFL MVP Boomer
20 Film director Nicolas
22 Off-color
23 ___ friends
25 Louisiana feature
27 Editorial cartoonist Hulme
31 Name meaning "heavenly"
33 Jr. and sr.
34 Bud in Burgundy
35 Iranian city
36 Snapshot, for short
37 Grammatical mood
40 To the right, maybe
41 Red dye
42 Cong. period
43 Bother no end: 2 wds.

Down

1 Kind of sharp wit
2 Opera singer Caruso
3 Slight feeling, as of regret
4 U.S.A.F. weapon
5 Cousin of a loon
6 Stock or C.D.: abbr.
7 Div. including the Braves and Marlins: 2 wds.
8 Bottle used for holding acids
9 Grown dearer in price
11 Relating to the action of the wind
13 Fail to take advantage of (a chance): 3 wds.
19 Four-time Pro Bowl tight end Crumpler
21 "I'll Be Doggone" singer, 1965
24 Muslim place of worship
25 Addle

26 Courtroom defenses
28 Keyboard user
29 Information of little importance
30 Way up
31 Houses, in Spain
32 Pageant host
38 Certain law degrees, initially
39 "A View ____ Kill" (James Bond film): 2 wds.

35

Across

1. "Lunar Asparagus" sculptor Max
6. Kevin who played a small-screen Hercules
11. Dove, at times
12. Render defenseless
13. Brooklyn's ___ Island
14. Last name that means "kings" in Spanish
15. Additive used to stabilize processed foods
17. Make hard and strong
18. "Lord, is ___?": Matthew: 2 wds.
19. Small stream
23. Mink cousin
26. Hebrew letter: var.
27. Tiny: var.
29. Sch. in Athens or its bulldog mascot
30. Household hints columnist
33. Going backwards
36. Bull: prefix
37. Philanthropist
38. Syria's Hafez-al-___

39. "Fighting vainly the old ___": Cole Porter
40. Watery milk parts
41. Russian objections

Down

1. "Behold," to Caesar
2. Small, enclosed place
3. Not attached to an org. of workers
4. Makes blind, as a falcon
5. Secret get-together
6. Glut, excess
7. Playwright Eugene and former House Speaker Tip
8. "Hellzapoppin'" actress Martha
9. ___ Rabbit (Harris character)
10. Mantra syllables
16. Occupational ending
18. British verb ending
20. Swiss town on the north shore of Lake Geneva
21. Narrowly defeated: 2 wds.
22. Mad Hatter's drink

24 Receptacle used by smokers

25 Auto parts: 2 wds.

28 "Telephone Line" band, for short

31 Epigram pro Nash

32 It may feature a twist

33 Foolhardy

34 Suffix with chant or mass

35 Discordia's Greek counterpart

36 Seen, to Tweety

36

Across

1 Feature of some pants
6 Toronto-based network
9 Empty
11 "V for Vendetta" actor Stephen
12 Self-indulgent activity: 2 wds.
14 Weather org.
15 Brief time out?
16 22.5 degrees, initially
17 Hearty "ha, ha, ha"
18 Extra-point score
19 Fatty, as tissue
21 Prefix with meter
22 "Why should ___ you?": 2 wds.
23 Tip on a weapon
26 Old-fashioned knife
27 Not quite on cloud nine
28 Disciple of 26-down
30 They get you into a concert, casually
33 Middle East political letters
34 Sound of hesitation
35 Actress Hagen
36 Football center?
37 Nutty
39 German pronoun
40 English poet Dowson
41 Majors or Myles
42 Farm refrain

Down

1 Benzene (prefix)
2 Boston airport
3 Run off to the preacher
4 PC key
5 Twister
6 Big name in coloring
7 Filled with bewilderment
8 Small box for holding valuables
10 Blind: 2 wds.
13 Can. province
20 The ___ Piper of Hamelin
21 Cookie since 1912
23 Oily liquid used in synthetic dyes
24 Compunction

25 Erratic

26 The Apostle of the Gentiles: 2 wds.

29 City in "The Lost Princess of Oz"

30 Student getting one-on-one help

31 Formal response to "Who's there?": 3 wds.

32 Kind of knife: hyph.

38 Secretive maritime org.

37

Across

1 Nest noises
7 Canceled: 2 wds.
11 Joseph of "Citizen Kane"
12 Spanish eyes
13 Llama relative
14 Large hall
15 Article in Die Zeit
16 Charley Weaver's hometown: abbr., 2 wds.
17 100 lbs.
19 Primeval giant of Norse mythology
21 Furrow maker
22 It works like a charm
26 Orderly grouping
29 Third stomach of a ruminant
30 Day-____
31 Celeb
33 Mindreader's claim, for short
34 Clarkson and Wachowski
37 Prince Valiant's son
39 Optimistic credo: 2 wds.
40 Sourly, tartly
43 Conspiracy
44 Issue an edict
45 Yorkshire river
46 Dr. Jekyll's counterpart: 2 wds.

Down

1 Half of CDX
2 ____ polloi
3 Yadda yadda yadda: 2 wds.
4 Pincushion alternative
5 Marshall of "Awakenings"
6 White stuff in Edinburgh
7 Quack's medicine
8 City in Ventura County
9 Metal, atomic number 79
10 "____ can you see": 2 wds.
16 Charade
17 Labor Secretary Elaine ____
18 Soil-dwelling invertebrate
20 Rolling rock
23 Handed down stories
24 Some blowups: abbr.
25 Sporty car roof: hyph.
27 Armand of "The Whole World at Our Feet"
28 Loco

32 Soap Box Derby entrant
34 Cosmetic surgery procedure, briefly
35 Anti-censorship gp.
36 Inner cell of an ancient temple
38 Deep
40 Fleet runner: abbr.
41 Fronted
42 "____-haw!"

38

Across

1 Get good, as with a tackle in football
5 Homebuilder's strip
9 "Check Yes ___" (George Strait song): 2 wds.
10 First word of a counting rhyme
11 "Miami Vice" cop ___ Tubbs
12 "___ a Broken Heart" (Bon Jovi song): 2 wds.
13 Wisconsin city
15 Anjou alternative
16 Med. dose
20 "It ___ lot to me": 2 wds.
22 Wide widths, initially
23 Zidovudine, familiarly
24 Clearblue competitor
26 Jimjams, initially
27 Ethnic group of Ethiopia
29 Lively intelligence
31 Maori war god
32 Wife of Shiva
33 Gave a glare: 2 wds.
37 Money paid out
40 Skateboarding footwear and clothing company
41 Stock car driver
42 Spanish muralist
43 "___ ever so humble, …": 2 wds.
44 Lover of Ares in Greek mythology

Down

1 Scand. country
2 Cantatrice's offering
3 Apparatus for hatching eggs
4 Be an observer: 2 wds.
5 Emissary
6 Suffix with meth or prop
7 Familia member
8 Playmate selector, familiarly
10 Anglo-Saxon letter in the form of a crossed 'D'
12 Panic button for computer users: 2 wds.
14 90° from norte
17 Laid up
18 Alien life watchers org.
19 "Hey!"
20 Wing, say

21 "The Snowy Day" author ___ Jack Keats
25 Ivan or Nicholas
28 Missile fired from a gun
30 "The magic word"
34 Musical sense
35 Gossamer
36 Baum barker
37 Eye
38 Oil-rich federation, initially
39 1999 AT&T purchase

39

Across

1 Olden drum
6 Subcontracts, with "out"
11 ___ null (set theory concept)
12 Construction piece: hyph.
13 Certain école
14 Dark red edible seaweed
15 Exactly: 3 wds.
17 Edinburgh man's hat
19 Snitched
20 Sponsorship: var.
22 Tiara
26 News hr., for some: 2 wds.
28 Sleep loudly
29 Get back
31 Contemptible one
32 Boast
34 N.F.L. linemen: abbr.
35 Highest floor on a ship: 2 wds.
39 Replay camera, for short: hyph.
40 Classical architecture style
43 Relating to a hair

44 Anti-Parkinson's drug: hyph.
45 Connery, Combs, et al.
46 "Rio" singer Simon: 2 wds.

Down

1 "She's So High" singer Bachman
2 Hayworth's hubby ___ Khan
3 Developing into
4 Break the seal
5 Butler in "Gone With the Wind"
6 "Semper ___" (Marine's motto)
7 Plentiful
8 Move, in real estate slang
9 Physics calculation
10 Hook's "right hand"
16 Mason's burden
17 Four: prefix
18 "A Death in the Family" playwright James
21 Astronaut
23 Handle

24 Q.E.D. part
25 Club ___ (resorts)
27 Eisoptrophobe's fear
30 Doze (off)
33 "One Touch of Venus" composer
35 Snail-mail system, initially
36 Dance move
37 Silents star Negri
38 The "C" in U.P.C.
41 Stock letters
42 Cooler

1

Across: 1 Orbs, 5 It's so, 10 Harm, 11 Loreal, 12 Omoo,
13 Alamos, 14 Hawk-eyed, 16 Nene, 17 Espy, 21 Warder, 23 Rtes,
24 Ami, 25 Are, 26 Foch, 28 Cotter, 31 Tyee, 32 Eyre, 33 Analysis,
37 Chorus, 40 I'm on, 41 Cup tie, 42 Nano, 43 Crest, 44 Gnaw.
Down: 1 Oh-oh, 2 Rama, 3 Brown rice, 4 Smoked, 5 Iole,
6 Trader, 7 Sem, 8 Sao, 9 OLs, 11 Layer, 15 ENE, 18 Statesman,
19 Pere, 20 Yser, 21 Waft, 22 Amoy, 27 Hearts, 28 Cease, 29 Oyl,
30 Trying, 34 Nuit, 35 Iona, 36 Snow, 37 CCC, 38 Hur, 39 Ope.

2

Across: 1 Govs, 5 Hops, 9 I lied, 11 Olson, 13 Ferri, 14 Say-so,
15 Tog, 16 Eda, 18 Con, 19 Eli, 20 Urn, 21 Hoe, 22 Dens,
24 Unions, 26 Fan mail, 28 Slocum, 30 Noir, 33 Har, 34 Cen,
36 Goo, 37 Ome, 38 LRG, 39 IDs, 40 Jesse, 42 Op cit, 44 Intra,
45 Shane, 46 Tsar, 47 Iler.
Down: 1 Gifted, 2 Ole ole, 3 Virgin forests, 4 Ser, 5 Hosanna,
6 Ola, 7 Psychological, 8 So soon, 10 Dieu, 12 Nones,
17 Drummer, 23 Sac, 25 I in, 27 Nuclear, 28 Shoji, 29 Lament,
31 Iodine, 32 Roster, 35 NGOs, 41 Sra, 43 Phi.

3

Across: 1 Holst, 6 Nooks, 11 I see a, 12 Ender, 13 Elman,
14 Muirs, 15 Doorkeeper, 17 Noses, 18 SCTV, 20 Circus,
25 Snees, 27 Selah, 28 Snares, 30 Aery, 31 Theda,
33 Top bananas, 38 Nilla, 39 Spots, 40 Indic, 41 U-turn, 42 Hasek,
43 Estas.

Down: 1 Hied, 2 Oslo, 3 Lemon tea, 4 Sea rover, 5 Tanks, 6 Nemesis, 7 On Up, 8 Odie, 9 Kerr, 10 Srs, 16 EEC, 18 Sss, 19 CNN, 21 Readapts, 22 Clean out, 23 UAR, 24 Shy, 26 Setback, 29 Sha, 32 Ensue, 33 Tina, 34 Olds, 35 Plie, 36 Atra, 37 SSNs, 38 NIH.

4

Across: 1 Emeril, 7 Sabe, 11 Bishop, 12 Worn, 13 Encountered, 15 Roods, 16 Eat at, 17 Lara, 18 Enrico, 19 Ent, 20 Snatch, 21 It's No, 22 Fan out, 24 Nam, 27 Fickle, 28 Bike, 29 Laila, 30 Sober, 31 Indefinable, 33 NCIS, 34 Teslas, 35 'Tecs, 36 Detest.

Down: 1 Eberle, 2 Minoan, 3 Escort, 4 Rhoda, 5 IOUs, 6 LPN, 7 Swear to, 8 Aortic, 9 Breach, 10 End to, 14 Tenant, 18 Ensue, 20 St Olaf, 21 Inkless, 22 Fiancé, 23 Acidic, 24 Nibble, 25 Akelas, 26 Merest, 27 Flint, 28 Boast, 30 Snee, 32 It'd.

5

Across: 1 It is, 5 Hit me, 10 Mont, 11 Unwon, 12 FIFA, 13 Mr Toad, 14 A due, 16 Ews, 17 Peninsula, 20 Catalog, 21 Yak, 24 TCP, 25 AMA, 26 MSN, 27 Shr, 28 Cordite, 30 Overthrow, 32 Ade, 33 Pear, 34 Chinch, 36 Roni, 39 Magus, 40 Mr Ed, 41 Abyss, 42 Ashe.

Down: 1 IMF, 2 Toi, 3 Infant prodigy, 4 Stadia, 5 Hur, 6 Intel, 7 Two-way mirrors, 8 Moas, 9 End, 13 Mesomorph, 15 Unlace, 17 Pcts, 18 Each, 19 Ugarte, 22 As to, 23 Knew, 29 Dharma, 31 Venus, 32 Ahab, 34 CMA, 35 CSs, 37 Neh, 38 Ide.

6

Across: 1 C-clamp, 7 ATM, 10 One inch, 11 NWA,
12 Soda cracker, 14 At an, 15 Rolen, 16 Gere, 17 Impede, 18 Ess,
19 Starts, 20 Mecca, 21 Apathy, 23 BSA, 26 Friday, 27 Neut,
28 Accts, 29 Also, 30 Shaving foam, 33 Ter, 34 Destiny, 35 SRO,
36 E-boats.

Down: 1 C-notes, 2 Cedars, 3 Liane, 4 ANC, 5 Mcr, 6 Pharmacy,
7 Anklet, 8 Tweeds, 9 Marne, 10 Osage, 13 Copra, 17 Itchy,
19 Set aside, 20 Mad TV, 21 Archer, 22 Picaro, 23 Beloit,
24 Susans, 25 Atomy, 26 Fasts, 27 NAFTA, 31 Neb, 32 GSO.

7

Across: 1 BOAC, 5 Age gap, 11 Inga, 12 Pedals, 13 Tourist trap,
15 Oranges, 16 Easement, 21 Jails, 24 Taros, 25 Agni, 26 Kata,
27 Macao, 29 Aesir, 30 Blandish, 32 Inwards, 36 Leisure suit,
40 Genome, 41 Thad, 42 Egoism, 43 Ergs.

Down: 1 Bit-o, 2 On or, 3 Agua, 4 Carnelian, 5 Apses, 6 Get set,
7 EDT, 8 Gar, 9 Ala, 10 PSP, 14 IGAs, 17 Make haste, 18 Eras,
19 Not I, 20 Tsar, 21 Jamb, 22 A Gal, 23 Inca, 28 Odiums,
29 As we, 31 In rem, 33 Ruhr, 34 Diag, 35 Stds, 36 Lge, 37 EEG,
38 Ino, 39 So I.

8

Across: 1 Maru, 5 A dio, 9 Plano, 11 Smell, 12 GEICO, 13 Pokes,
14 Namers, 16 RSSs, 18 Nantes, 22 Utterly, 24 Hal, 25 Mao,
26 UAE, 27 Esa, 28 Brr, 29 Irrupts, 31 Arming, 33 Nosh,
34 Koenig, 36 Do You, 39 Adult, 42 Ivans, 43 Sleds, 44 Sews,
45 Esse.

Down: 1 MPG, 2 Ale, 3 Rainstorm, 4 Uncase, 5 Amos 'n', 6 Dek, 7 Ile, 8 OLs, 10 Oom, 11 Sprayer, 15 Enlarge, 16 Rumba, 17 Starr, 19 The Pogues, 20 Easts, 21 Slash, 23 Ruinous, 30 Unidle, 32 Ikons, 35 Nas, 36 Dis, 37 Ove, 38 Yaw, 40 LDS, 41 Tse.

9

Across: 1 Lad, 4 Celine, 10 Open, 12 Look on, 13 Greg, 14 Encode, 15 Espana, 17 Fiori, 19 RBH, 22 Coronas, 24 ELO, 25 An I, 26 Und, 27 Pun, 28 Mme, 29 Scolari, 31 OED, 32 Eensy, 33 Seamus, 36 Ramada, 41 Tete, 42 Bethel, 43 Snee, 44 I raise, 45 Tps.

Down: 1 Loge, 2 Aprs, 3 Deep-fried, 4 Clearance sale, 5 Eon, 6 Loc, 7 Iko, 8 Nod, 9 ENE, 11 Ngaio, 16 Nonuse, 18 Is Done, 19 Repayment, 20 Blur, 21 Honi, 22 Camo, 23 On me, 30 LSATs, 34 UTEP, 35 Sees, 36 RBI, 37 Aer, 38 MTA, 39 Ahi, 40 Des.

10

Across: 1 Mad TV, 6 Pho, 9 Store, 10 Those, 12 Enlisted man, 14 Coe, 15 Tia, 16 Eye, 17 Hillel, 19 Mirage, 22 Tail, 25 Aleve, 26 Canto, 27 Is so, 28 Top dog, 29 Octave, 31 AOL, 33 Ire, 34 Via, 37 Thunderbolt, 40 Totsy, 41 Usurp, 42 Hew, 43 Pases.

Down: 1 M sec, 2 At no, 3 Dole, 4 Tri, 5 Vestige, 6 PhD, 7 Homeland, 8 O say, 10 Teal, 11 ENE, 13 Tile, 17 Havoc, 18 Etape, 19 Mai, 20 Ils, 21 Resolute, 23 I to, 24 Log, 26 Cover-up, 28 Tare, 30 Tidy, 31 ATT, 32 Oh-oh, 34 Vous, 35 Il re, 36 Atps, 38 NSW, 39 BSA.

11

Across: 1 Resow, 6 Frond, 11 Oribi, 12 Renee, 13 Box in, 14 Eleve, 15 Tessa, 17 I am, 18 Lee, 20 Orkan, 22 A-teams, 24 Badu, 27 Ounce, 28 Leman, 29 Sith, 30 Iodine, 31 Henny, 33 Lgs, 34 Run, 36 Stall, 38 Choky, 40 Lying, 43 Put on, 44 Trout, 45 The OC, 46 Yanni.

Down: 1 Rob, 2 Ero, 3 Sixteenth note, 4 Obie, 5 Winsome, 6 Freak, 7 Rel, 8 One in a million, 9 Neva, 10 Deem, 16 Srs, 18 Laos, 19 Etui, 21 Abed, 23 Ache, 25 Dang, 26 Unes, 28 Loyalty, 30 Int, 32 NSYNC, 34 Rcpt, 35 Uh-uh, 37 Lyra, 39 Koo, 41 Nun, 42 GTI.

12

Across: 1 Obits, 6 Ests, 10 Nonet, 11 Scion, 12 Softy, 13 Today, 14 Phi, 15 Lau, 17 ETD, 18 Eon, 19 ESD, 20 See, 21 Coir, 23 Kipper, 25 Topsoil, 27 Reek of, 29 Rise, 32 Hds, 33 LOL, 35 THI, 36 Oui, 37 Ira, 38 Tal, 39 Mamas, 41 Seine, 43 Brash, 44 Innie, 45 Idle, 46 Kagan.

Down: 1 On spec, 2 Boohoo, 3 Infinitesimal, 4 Tet, 5 Style, 6 Eco, 7 Sidesplitting, 8 To a tee, 9 Snyder, 11 Studio, 16 Asks for, 22 ROK, 24 Pi R, 26 Polish, 27 Rhombi, 28 Eduard, 30 Shania, 31 Eileen, 34 Lasik, 40 Ase, 42 Ena.

13

Across: 1 Much, 5 On CDs, 10 Oprah, 12 Dozen, 13 Opere, 14 Otero, 15 Lim, 16 AAA, 18 Car, 19 Ate, 20 Luc, 21 Hit, 22 Hyde, 24 Pearls, 26 En garde, 28 Armani, 30 A par, 33 Dee, 34 Arb, 36 Udo, 37 USN, 38 SSA, 39 Boa, 40 Letch, 42 Kilns, 44 Te-hee, 45 Uniat, 46 Snees, 47 Acis.

1 Moolah, 2 Uppity, 3 Crème de menthe, 4 Har, 5 Odoacer, 6 Not, 7 Czech Republic, 8 Derail, 9 Snorts, 11 Heal, 17 Au pairs, 23 Ena, 25 Ada, 27 Gnashes, 28 Adults, 29 Reseen, 31 Adonai, 32 Roasts, 35 Baku, 41 Cee, 43 In a.

14

Across: 1 A dog, 5 Space, 10 Devo, 11 Rail at, 12 Ice-T, 13 Oxcart, 14 Marilu, 16 Knee, 17 Stigma, 19 DDE, 21 That's it, 25 He a, 26 OSS, 27 Isl, 28 Lash-ups, 30 DSC, 31 O'Toole, 33 Ali G, 36 Knowns, 39 Beetle, 41 Gila, 42 Assign, 43 I Ten, 44 Tetes, 45 NHRA.

Down: 1 A dim, 2 Deca, 3 Overseas, 4 Got it, 5 Sax, 6 Pick at, 7 Alan, 8 Care, 9 Ette, 11 Rough-spoken, 15 Lit out, 18 Masson, 19 DHL, 20 Dea, 22 Side with, 23 Iss, 24 TLC, 29 Hog-tie, 32 Log in, 33 A bat, 34 Lese, 35 Iest, 37 NLer, 38 Sana, 40 Lgs.

15

Across: 1 Ran in, 6 Price, 11 Orono, 12 Retow, 13 Miss M, 14 Erase, 15 Pepsi-Cola, 17 Bagnio, 18 Ivan, 20 F-stops, 24 Bon, 25 Kae, 26 Neu, 27 Madden, 29 Ecce, 30 On tour, 32 Many-sided, 35 Patna, 36 Lodes, 38 US ten, 39 Eries, 40 Stars, 41 Dates.

Down: 1 ROM, 2 A rip, 3 Noseband, 4 Inspan, 5 No MSG, 6 Precise, 7 Reroot, 8 Ital, 9 Cosa, 10 Ewe, 16 Infants, 18 IBM, 19 VOA, 21 On credit, 22 Pec, 23 Sue, 25 Kenyans, 28 Donner, 29 Eudora, 31 Oiled, 32 Mast, 33 Atta, 34 Deee, 35 Pus, 37 Sss.

16

Across: 1 Olafs, 6 Skosh, 11 Magic, 12 Lacto, 13 Open-hearted, 15 Odea, 16 Lia, 17 Gauntlet, 22 Uralic, 25 ENE, 26 Superimpose, 29 MFA, 30 Delved, 31 Africana, 34 Lat, 35 Sloe, 39 Residential, 43 Ether, 44 Milks, 45 Laude, 46 Icosa.

Down: 1 Omoo, 2 LAPD, 3 Agee, 4 Finagle, 5 Sch, 6 Slain, 7 Karat, 8 Oct, 9 Ste, 10 Hod, 14 Elucidate, 18 Air, 19 Leo V, 20 Ense, 21 Teed, 22 USMA, 23 Ruff, 24 A par, 27 Men, 28 Plastic, 32 I lied, 33 Cadre, 36 Lilo, 37 Oaks, 38 Elsa, 39 Rel, 40 Eta, 41 Shu, 42 NMI.

17

Across: 1 Niche, 6 Gra, 9 Anoint, 11 Toed, 12 Shaped, 13 Eat a, 14 Cash, 15 Sendup, 17 Alti, 18 Anent, 19 Resp, 20 Brides, 21 Hails, 23 Sarong, 26 RISC, 30 A Riot, 31 Alpe, 32 Lab rat, 34 Clan, 35 ABAA, 36 Hikers, 38 Ally, 39 In esse, 40 Med, 41 Otter.

Down: 1 NASCAR, 2 Inhale, 3 Coasts, 4 Hip hip hooray, 5 ENE, 6 Goaded, 7 Retune, 8 Adapts, 10 Tds, 11 Tennis racket, 16 Earl, 20 Big, 22 Anta, 23 Salaam, 24 Arable, 25 Ribald, 27 Illest, 28 Sparse, 29 Censer, 33 THI, 37 Ino.

18

Across: 1 Egale, 6 Beam, 10 Lupin, 11 Asset, 13 Violoncello, 15 Eal, 16 Loc, 17 Ote, 18 RNA, 19 S-shaped, 21 Sara, 23 Euler, 24 Pabst, 26 Cupel, 28 Alpe, 32 Wastrel, 34 URL, 35 Ere, 36 OEO, 37 Sea, 38 Aides-de-camp, 41 Retro, 42 Wakes, 43 Soil, 44 Evade.

Down: 1 Elvers, 2 Guiana, 3 Apolar, 4 Lil, 5 Enols, 6 Bacchus, 7 Ese, 8 Aslope, 9 Melter, 12 Toed, 14 Nosebleed, 20 Alta, 22 Appt, 25 Aerosol, 26 Caries, 27 Used to, 29 Lusaka, 30 Premed, 31 Elapse, 32 Wear, 33 Loewe, 39 Eri, 40 Cav.

19

Across: 1 Tased, 6 Scone, 11 Acute, 12 Oil up, 13 Debts, 14 Anais, 15 Adjustment, 17 Emir, 18 Suvari, 22 Arms, 26 Op art, 27 MMXII, 28 Banc, 29 Season, 30 Hall, 32 Redecorate, 38 Not us, 39 Depot, 40 Ricki, 41 In bad, 42 Asher, 43 Cists.

Down: 1 Ta-da, 2 Aced, 3 Subj, 4 Et tu, 5 Dessert, 6 So am I, 7 Cinerama, 8 Olan, 9 Nuit, 10 EPs, 16 TMI, 18 Sob, 19 Up a, 20 Van, 21 Archduke, 23 Rxs, 24 MiO, 25 Sin, 27 Melodic, 29 SLC, 31 Aesir, 32 Rois, 33 Etch, 34 Reni, 35 APBs, 36 To a T, 37 ETDs, 38 NRA.

20

Across: 1 ETDs, 5 In a row, 11 Shun, 12 Nettle, 13 Toni, 14 Tab set, 15 A neg, 16 Ola, 17 Blat, 19 Trou, 23 Glues on, 26 ERs, 27 Leg to, 28 Assoc, 30 Ang, 31 Killing, 33 Days, 35 Maud, 36 HMO, 38 Memo, 41 Kopeck, 44 Bnai, 45 I Need a, 46 Eccl, 47 Dearly, 48 Rees.

Down: 1 Esta, 2 Thon, 3 Dune buggy, 4 Sniglet, 5 In toto, 6 Neal, 7 At bat, 8 Rts, 9 Ole, 10 Wet, 18 Asok, 20 Residence, 21 Or on, 22 USCG, 23 Glad, 24 Lena, 25 Nala, 29 Slumber, 32 I'm okay, 34 Sheer, 37 MCDL, 39 Mace, 40 Oils, 41 Kid, 42 One, 43 Pea.

21

Across: 1 Bitmap, 7 Ten, 10 Erhard, 11 HBO, 12 Wheelbarrow, 14 Hondas, 15 AAAA, 16 Olea, 17 Misty, 18 MDs, 19 Keiths, 21 Filet, 22 T-Birds, 24 Tso, 27 Memos, 28 Dian, 29 Uxor, 30 Omasum, 32 Saving grace, 34 Ici, 35 Ermine, 36 Coe, 37 Vetoer.

Down: 1 Behold, 2 Irenes, 3 Theda, 4 Mala, 5 Arbs, 6 PDA, 7 Thrash, 8 E-boats, 9 No way, 12 Whom, 13 Raitt, 17 Mies, 19 Kirs, 20 Eld, 21 Fiori, 22 Texaco, 23 B-movie, 24 Tisane, 25 Saucer, 26 On me, 27 Music, 28 Dario, 30 Ogre, 31 MGMT, 33 Nev.

22

Across: 1 Waul, 5 Amas, 9 Epson, 11 Vase, 12 Blank verse, 14 Con, 15 Ginseng, 17 AMC, 18 Btu, 19 Rte, 20 MBEs, 22 Rector, 24 Alibi, 26 Goo-goo, 29 Edy's, 33 Exp, 34 RLS, 36 Evo, 37 Stearin, 39 Ker, 40 Anticipate, 42 Ilie, 43 Pelts, 44 Lyes, 45 I bet.

Down: 1 Webcam, 2 Aplomb, 3 Usance, 4 Lon, 5 Avenue B, 6 Mars, 7 Assert, 8 Seen to, 10 NKGB, 13 Vitriolic, 16 Ger, 21 Sag, 23 Cie, 25 Lorries, 26 GEs, 27 Oxtail, 28 Openly, 30 De Kalb, 31 Yvette, 32 Sorest, 35 Snip, 38 A tie, 41 Pei.

23

Across: 1 Grappa, 7 ACA, 10 Redraw, 11 Flav, 12 Eureka, 13 Lyme, 14 Asis, 15 Geyser, 17 Seve, 18 Lisas, 19 Eden, 20 Donate, 21 Twang, 23 Square, 26 Seis, 30 Tante, 31 Axle, 32 Atkins, 34 UCLA, 35 Mano, 36 Racism, 38 Pron, 39 Ice tea, 40 Sit, 41 Street.

Down: 1 Grease, 2 Reused, 3 A drive, 4 Presentation, 5 Pak, 6 Awag, 7 Alyssa, 8 Came at, 9 Averse, 11 Flying saucer, 16 Elon, 20 Dae, 22 Wren, 23 Stamps, 24 Qatari, 25 Unknot, 27 Excite, 28 I'll see, 29 Sea mat, 33 Sris, 37 Act.

24

Across: 1 Educ, 5 Gas cap, 11 Rash, 12 Thorpe, 13 Indigestion, 15 Clare, 16 Hess, 17 Reinas, 20 Arfs, 23 F-stops, 26 Gel, 27 Hic, 28 USA, 29 Seal it, 31 Util, 32 Gets in, 34 Nape, 36 Espoo, 40 E Howard Hunt, 43 Malawi, 44 Opie, 45 Obeyed, 46 Data.

Down: 1 Eric, 2 Danl, 3 USDA, 4 Chirrs, 5 GTE, 6 Ahs, 7 So that, 8 Cries out, 9 APOs, 10 Pens, 14 Gee, 18 If It's, 19 NSC, 20 AGs, 21 Ree, 22 Flagpole, 24 Psi, 25 Sal, 27 Hit, 30 Leeway, 31 Unshod, 33 IED, 34 Nemo, 35 Ahab, 37 Pupa, 38 On it, 39 'Ote'a, 41 Awe, 42 Rid.

25

Across: 1 In F, 4 AFB, 7 TAE, 8 Tru, 9 Gnu, 12 CPR, 13 Margret, 15 Horns, 17 Pooch, 18 Elia, 19 Duce, 20 Dishrag, 24 Nor, 25 Wayward, 27 Ohh, 29 End user, 32 Toed, 34 Etna, 35 Tweak, 37 Osric, 38 Oil pans, 40 Ose, 41 Ses, 42 Tah, 43 KLM, 44 An I, 45 EEE.

Down: 1 Itched, 2 Napoli, 3 Ferris wheels, 4 ATMs, 5 Fra, 6 Burp, 9 Ground stroke, 10 Necco, 11 Uther, 14 God, 16 Naha, 21 Rye, 22 Awn, 23 Gad, 26 Rues, 27 Ottos, 28 Howie, 30 Enisle, 31 Raceme, 33 Dap, 36 Kata, 37 Oshi, 39 Nan.

26

Across: 1 Arrows, 7 Sharona, 9 SAE, 12 Hemlock, 13 Ern, 14 Ebb, 15 Collie, 17 Rough, 20 No for, 21 Knout, 23 Opto, 24 Comes to, 26 Retd, 28 Tiers, 30 Anils, 32 Erte's, 34 Lloyd's, 36 Rea, 37 Pau, 38 Anoraks, 41 His, 42 Kiddies, 43 Pastry.

Down: 1 Asher, 2 Rhebok, 3 Rambunctious, 4 ORL, 5 Woo, 6 SNCC, 8 Akon, 9 Self-portrait, 10 A Riot, 11 Enero, 16 Looter, 18 Goodly, 19 Hum, 22 Tet, 25 Sie, 26 Ralph, 27 Enlai, 29 Seeker, 31 S Dak, 33 Sassy, 35 Snip, 39 Oda, 40 Rds.

27

Across: 1 Cried, 6 Ghia, 10 Rarer, 11 A bent, 12 Adolescence, 14 Mab, 15 GWU, 16 Baa, 17 Browser, 19 Ism, 20 Oste, 21 Earth's, 23 Betsy, 25 Accede, 28 NASA, 32 Bor, 33 Inverts, 35 An E, 36 Tee, 37 Go's, 38 C major scale, 41 Aesir, 42 Talls, 43 B neg, 44 Amies.

Down: 1 Crambo, 2 Radars, 3 I Robot, 4 Eel, 5 Dregs, 6 GBE, 7 Henbit, 8 In cash, 9 A-teams, 11 Acuras, 13 Sweetener, 18 We be, 22 Ryne, 24 Editor, 25 Abacab, 26 Con men, 27 Crease, 29 Argali, 30 Stolle, 31 Assess, 34 Vesta, 39 Jig, 40 Cam.

28

Across: 1 Unes, 5 Awards, 11 So to, 12 Noters, 13 Maru, 14 Deceit, 15 Cherry Bomb, 17 Cleese, 18 Gamest, 21 Trio, 24 DNA, 25 Gan, 26 Size, 28 Emmett, 31 Elixir, 33 Plantation, 37 Ultimo, 38 Oaky, 39 Nooner, 40 Ager, 41 Advent, 42 Dodo.

Down: 1 USMC, 2 Noah, 3 Etre, 4 Source, 5 And yet, 6 Woe be, 7 At cost, 8 Reemerge, 9 Drib, 10 SST, 16 RLS, 18 Gds, 19 Ani, 20 Mazeltov, 22 I at, 23 Ont, 27 Elaine, 28 Extort, 29 Mia, 30 Mr Toad, 32 In men, 33 Plod, 34 Iago, 35 Ok'ed, 36 Nyro, 37 Una.

29

Across: 1 A few, 5 Thermo, 11 Leah, 12 Rabbit, 13 Vero, 14 Albino, 15 Atty, 16 Passes, 17 Hoops, 19 Demure, 21 Dow, 24 Ode, 25 Urb, 27 Ela, 28 E'en, 29 Job jar, 31 Lorre, 32 Says ah, 36 Acid, 39 Unworn, 40 NTSB, 41 Vacuum, 42 Dell, 43 Staled, 44 Odas.

Down: 1 Alva, 2 Feet, 3 Earthmen, 4 Who you,
5 Trapper John MD, 6 Halas, 7 Ebbs, 8 RBIs, 9 Mine, 10 Otos,
18 ORU, 19 Doe, 20 Ede, 21 Dejected, 22 Ola, 23 War, 26 Bor,
30 Brando, 31 LaRue, 32 SUVs, 33 Anat, 34 YWCA, 35 Soul,
37 Isla, 38 Dbls.

30

Across: 1 Islip, 6 Mead, 10 Guava, 11 Ypres, 13 Uncertainty,
15 Edu, 16 Col, 17 E'er, 18 Sandhog, 20 TCI, 21 Sear, 22 Liotta,
24 Atman, 26 Balboa, 29 Evil, 33 Ava, 34 Skyline, 36 Len, 37 Tee,
38 RSA, 39 Declaration, 42 Snead, 43 Salle, 44 Otra, 45 Tweed.
Down: 1 I guess, 2 Sundae, 3 Lacuna, 4 I've, 5 Parch, 6 Myalgia,
7 Epi, 8 Arnett, 9 Detect, 12 Syria, 14 Toolmaker, 19 Drab,
23 One L, 25 Tostada, 26 Balds, 27 Aveeno, 28 Lancet, 30 Virile,
31 Insole, 32 Leaned, 35 Yeast, 40 Lar, 41 Taw.

31

Across: 1 Nab, 4 Brr, 7 Ela, 8 Mae, 9 Spa, 12 Website, 14 Ulu,
15 Anya, 16 I'll bet, 18 Techno, 20 Etui, 21 Allcomers, 23 TSR,
25 Oil, 26 Ram, 27 Scrawnier, 30 Haig, 31 Ansara, 34 Imaret,
36 Onos, 37 RPG, 38 Witless, 40 Tie, 41 Eos, 42 Ait, 43 Sna,
44 NES.
Down: 1 New at, 2 Alene, 3 Baby carriage, 4 BMI, 5 Ratiocination,
6 Reel, 9 Subterranean, 10 Pleura, 11 Autism, 13 Sahl, 17 LEM,
19 N Low, 22 Olin, 23 T-shirt, 24 Scampi, 28 Agr, 29 ESOL,
32 Rosie, 33 Assts, 35 Ewes, 39 TSA.

32

Across: 1 Aleta, 6 Sappy, 11 Lt Col, 12 Pelee, 13 Promo, 14 O rare, 15 SSN, 16 Manon, 18 Bang, 19 Ter, 22 Mercenary, 24 Mead, 26 Oise, 27 Assertion, 31 Agt, 32 Hulk, 33 Oriel, 35 Pam, 38 Olden, 40 Braga, 42 Buono, 43 Entry, 44 Esnes, 45 Tahoe.

Down: 1 Alps, 2 Ltrs, 3 Econ, 4 Tom, 5 Alomar, 6 Sponge, 7 Aero, 8 Plantain, 9 Per, 10 Yee, 17 ANC, 18 Bede, 20 ERs, 21 Rye, 22 Mastodon, 23 Nook, 24 Maa, 25 ESG, 28 Rhinos, 29 Tue, 30 I'll bet, 34 Rene, 35 Path, 36 Agro, 37 Maye, 38 OBE, 39 Lus, 41 RNA.

33

Across: 1 Ibos, 5 Acari, 10 Stale, 11 Bacon, 12 Aerie, 13 As can, 14 Error, 15 A sure, 16 Nays, 17 Ilks, 18 SNL, 19 Clint, 22 Tellurium, 25 Veeck, 26 Rey, 28 A pie, 30 SASE, 31 Dente, 33 Baths, 34 Aesir, 35 Elian, 36 Plods, 37 Amoco, 38 Tenet, 39 Minh.

Down: 1 Iterant, 2 Barry Levinson, 3 Olios, 4 Seer, 5 ABAA, 6 Cassini, 7 Acculturation, 8 Roark, 9 Innes, 10 Saens, 19 Cle, 20 Luc, 21 Irk, 23 Lee tide, 24 Meshach, 27 Yes no, 28 Adapt, 29 Peele, 30 Salmi, 32 Erst, 33 Beam.

34

Across: 1 Retag, 6 Incr, 10 Anwar, 11 Enlai, 12 Prime movers, 14 I in, 15 Bil, 16 Abe, 17 ECG, 18 Esiason, 20 Roeg, 22 Salty, 23 Among, 25 Bayou, 27 Etta, 31 Celeste, 33 Yrs, 34 Ami, 35 Qom, 36 Pic, 37 Subjunctive, 40 Aside, 41 Eosin, 42 Sess, 43 Eat at.

Down: 1 Rapier, 2 Enrico, 3 Twinge, 4 AAM, 5 Grebe, 6 Inv, 7 NL East, 8 Carboy, 9 Risen, 11 Eolian, 13 Miss out on, 19 Alge, 21 Gaye, 24 Mosque, 25 Bemuse, 26 Alibis, 28 Typist, 29 Trivia, 30 Ascent, 31 Casas, 32 Emcee, 38 JDs, 39 To a.

35

Across: 1 Ernst, 6 Sorbo, 11 Cooer, 12 Unarm, 13 Coney, 14 Reyes, 15 Emulsifier, 17 Ensteel, 18 It I, 19 Rillet, 23 Stoat, 26 Tsade, 27 Eensie, 29 UGA, 30 Heloise, 33 Retrograde, 36 Tauro, 37 Donor, 38 Assad, 39 Ennui, 40 Wheys, 41 Nyets.
Down: 1 Ecce, 2 Roomette, 3 Nonunion, 4 Seels, 5 Tryst, 6 Surfeit, 7 O'Neills, 8 Raye, 9 Brer, 10 Oms, 16 Ier, 18 Ise, 20 Lausanne, 21 Edged out, 22 Tea, 24 Ashtray, 25 Tie rods, 28 ELO, 31 Ogden, 32 Irony, 33 Rash, 34 Euse, 35 Eris, 36 Taw.

36

Across: 1 Pleat, 6 CBC, 9 Hollow, 11 Rea, 12 Ego trip, 14 AMS, 15 Nap, 16 NNE, 17 Yuk, 18 One, 19 Adipose, 21 Odo, 22 I let, 23 Arrowhead, 26 Snee, 27 Sad, 28 Timothy, 30 Tix, 33 PLO, 34 Haw, 35 Uta, 36 Air, 37 Idiotic, 39 Uns, 40 Ernest, 41 Lee, 42 EIEIO.
Down: 1 Pheno, 2 Logan, 3 Elope, 4 Alt, 5 Tornado, 6 Crayola, 7 Bemused, 8 Casket, 10 Window shade, 13 Pei, 20 Pied, 21 Oreo, 23 Aniline, 24 Remorse, 25 Haywire, 26 St Paul, 29 Thi, 30 Tutee, 31 It is I, 32 X-Acto, 38 ONI.

37

Across: 1 Cheeps, 7 No go, 11 Cotten, 12 Ojos, 13 Vicuna, 14 Sala, 15 Ein, 16 Mt Idy, 17 Cwt, 19 Ymir, 21 Hoe, 22 Amulet, 26 Arrangement, 29 Omasum, 30 Glo, 31 Star, 33 ESP, 34 Lanas, 37 Arn, 39 I can, 40 Acidly, 43 Plot, 44 Decree, 45 Ouse, 46 Mr Hyde.

Down: 1 CCV, 2 Hoi, 3 Et cetera, 4 Etui, 5 Penny, 6 Sna, 7 Nostrum, 8 Ojai, 9 Gold, 10 O say, 16 Mime, 17 Chao, 18 Worm, 20 Magma, 23 Legendry, 24 Enls, 25 T-top, 27 Assante, 28 Nuts, 32 Racer, 34 Lipo, 35 ACLU, 36 Naos, 38 Rich, 40 Adm, 41 Led, 42 Yee.

38

Across: 1 Nail, 5 Lath, 9 Or no, 10 Eenie, 11 Rico, 12 Edge of, 13 Waukesha, 15 Bosc, 16 Tbsp, 20 Meant a, 22 EEEs, 23 AZT, 24 EPT, 26 DTs, 27 Irob, 29 Esprit, 31 Maru, 32 Kali, 33 Leered at, 37 Outlay, 40 Adio, 41 Racer, 42 Sert, 43 Be it, 44 Enyo.

Down: 1 Norw, 2 Aria, 3 Incubator, 4 Look on, 5 Legate, 6 Ane, 7 Tio, 8 Hef, 10 Edh, 12 Escape key, 14 Este, 17 Bedridden, 18 Seti, 19 Psst, 20 Maim, 21 Ezra, 25 Tsar, 28 Bullet, 30 Please, 34 Ear, 35 Airy, 36 Toto, 37 Orb, 38 UAE, 39 TCI.

39

Across: 1 Tabor, 6 Farms, 11 Aleph, 12 I-beam, 13 Lycee, 14 Dulse, 15 On the nose, 17 Tam, 19 Told, 20 Egis, 22 Diadem, 26 Ten pm, 28 Snore, 29 Regain, 31 Toad, 32 Crow, 34 Rts, 35 Upper deck, 39 Slo-mo, 40 Ionic, 43 Pilar, 44 L-dopa, 45 Seans, 46 Le Bon.

Down: 1 Tal, 2 Aly, 3 Becoming, 4 Open, 5 Rhett, 6 Fidelis, 7 Abundant, 8 Relo, 9 Mass, 10 Smee, 16 Hod, 17 Tetr, 18 Agee, 21 Spaceman, 23 Doorknob, 24 Erat, 25 Meds, 27 Mirrors, 30 Nod, 33 Weill, 35 USPS, 36 Plie, 37 Pola, 38 Code, 41 IPO, 42 Can.